Harve

by Iain Gray

Lang**Syne**
PUBLISHING
WRITING *to* REMEMBER

Lang**Syne**

PUBLISHING

WRITING *to* REMEMBER

79 Main Street, Newtongrange,
Midlothian EH22 4NA
Tel: 0131 344 0414   Fax: 0845 075 6085
E-mail: info@lang-syne.co.uk
www.langsyneshop.co.uk

Design by Dorothy Meikle
Printed by Martins the Printers, Berwick-upon-Tweed
© Lang Syne Publishers Ltd 2013

ISBN 978-1-85217-516-0

Harvey

MOTTO:
Faith fears not.

CREST:
A demi-leopard.

NAME variations include:
Harvie
Hervey
Hervie

Chapter one:

The origins of popular surnames

by George Forbes and Iain Gray

If you don't know where you came from, you won't know where you're going **is a frequently quoted observation and one that has a particular resonance today when there has been a marked upsurge in interest in genealogy, with increasing numbers of people curious to trace their family roots.**

Main sources for genealogical research include census returns and official records of births, marriages and deaths – and the key to unlocking the detail they contain is obviously a family surname, one that has been 'inherited' and passed from generation to generation.

No matter our station in life, we all have a surname – but it was not until about the middle of the fourteenth century that the practice of being identified by a particular surname became commonly established throughout the British Isles.

Previous to this, it was normal for a person to be identified through the use of only a forename.

But as population gradually increased and there were many more people with the same forename, surnames were adopted to distinguish one person, or community, from another.

Many common English surnames are patronymic in origin, meaning they stem from the forename of one's father – with 'Johnson,' for example, indicating 'son of John.'

It was the Normans, in the wake of their eleventh century conquest of Anglo-Saxon England, a pivotal moment in the nation's history, who first brought surnames into usage – although it was a gradual process.

For the Normans, these were names initially based on the title of their estates, local villages and chateaux in France to distinguish and identify these landholdings.

Such grand descriptions also helped enhance the prestige of these warlords and generally glorify their lofty positions high above the humble serfs slaving away below in the pecking order who had only single names, often with Biblical connotations as in Pierre and Jacques.

The only descriptive distinctions among the peasantry concerned their occupations, like 'Pierre the swineherd' or 'Jacques the ferryman.'

Roots of surnames that came into usage in England not only included Norman-French, but also Old French, Old Norse, Old English, Middle English, German, Latin, Greek, Hebrew and the Gaelic languages of the Celts.

The Normans themselves were originally Vikings, or 'Northmen', who raided, colonised and eventually settled down around the French coastline.

The had sailed up the Seine in their longboats in 900AD under their ferocious leader Rollo and ruled the roost in north eastern France before sailing over to conquer England in 1066 under Duke William of Normandy – better known to posterity as William the Conqueror, or King William I of England.

Granted lands in the newly-conquered England, some of their descendants later acquired territories in Wales, Scotland and Ireland – taking not only their own surnames, but also the practice of adopting a surname, with them.

But it was in England where Norman rule and custom first impacted, particularly in relation to the adoption of surnames.

This is reflected in the famous *Domesday Book*, a massive survey of much of England and Wales, ordered by William I, to determine who owned what, what it was worth and therefore how much they were liable to pay in taxes to the voracious Royal Exchequer.

Completed in 1086 and now held in the National Archives in Kew, London, 'Domesday' was an Old English word meaning 'Day of Judgement.'

This was because, in the words of one contemporary chronicler, "its decisions, like those of the Last Judgement, are unalterable."

It had been a requirement of all those English landholders – from the richest to the poorest – that they identify themselves for the purposes of the survey and for future reference by means of a surname.

This is why the *Domesday Book*, although written in Latin as was the practice for several centuries with both civic and ecclesiastical records, is an invaluable source for the early appearance of a wide range of English surnames.

Several of these names were coined in connection with occupations.

These include Baker and Smith, while Cooks, Chamberlains, Constables and Porters were to be found carrying out duties in large medieval households.

The church's influence can be found in names such as Bishop, Friar and Monk while the popular name of Bennett derives from the late fifth to mid-sixth century Saint Benedict, founder of the Benedictine order of monks.

The early medical profession is represented by Barber, while businessmen produced names that include Merchant and Sellers.

Down at the village watermill, the names that cropped up included Millar/Miller, Walker and Fuller, while other self-explanatory trades included Cooper, Tailor, Mason and Wright.

Even the scenery was utilised as in Moor, Hill, Wood and Forrest – while the hunt and the chase supplied names that include Hunter, Falconer, Fowler and Fox.

Colours are also a source of popular surnames, as in Black, Brown, Gray/Grey, Green and White, and would have denoted the colour of the clothing the person habitually wore or, apart from the obvious exception of 'Green', one's hair colouring or even complexion.

The surname Red developed into Reid, while

Blue was rare and no-one wanted to be associated with yellow.

Rather self-important individuals took surnames that include Goodman and Wiseman, while physical attributes crept into surnames such as Small and Little.

Many families proudly boast the heraldic device known as a Coat of Arms, as featured on our front cover.

The central motif of the Coat of Arms would originally have been what was borne on the shield of a warrior to distinguish himself from others on the battlefield.

Not featured on the Coat of Arms, but high-lighted on page three, is the family motto and related crest – with the latter frequently different from the central motif.

Adding further variety to the rich cultural heritage that is represented by surnames is the appearance in recent times in lists of the 100 most common names found in England of ones that include Khan, Patel and Singh – names that have proud roots in the vast sub-continent of India.

Echoes of a far distant past can still be found in our surnames and they can be borne with pride in commemoration of our forebears.

Chapter two:

Invasion and conquest

**Derived from the Breton personal name 'Haervie',
'Harvey' and its popular spelling variants that
include 'Harvie' and 'Hervey' has ancient warlike
connotations.**

Stemming from 'haer', meaning 'battle' and
'vy' meaning 'worthy', the name in effect indicates
'battle-worthy.'

This is very apt, considering that the name
first came to British shores in the form of those Breton
mercenaries, from the area of modern-day Brittany in
north-west France, who accompanied Duke William
of Normandy in his 1066 Conquest of England.

In common with many other invaders,
however, their original bloodline mixed into a rich
and heady brew through intermarriage with the bloodlines of those indigenous people they had conquered.

This is why, despite the Breton/Norman roots
of the Harvey name, flowing through the veins of
many English bearers of the name today is also the
blood of Anglo-Saxons and even earlier settlers of the
British Isles.

Settling in the south and east of the island of Britain from about the early fifth century, the Anglo-Saxons were composed of the Jutes, from the area of the Jutland Peninsula in modern Denmark, the Saxons from Lower Saxony, in modern Germany and the Angles from the Angeln area of Germany.

It was the Angles who gave the name 'Engla land', or 'Aengla land' – better known as 'England.'

They held sway in what became known as England from approximately 550 to 1066, with the main kingdoms those of Sussex, Wessex, Northumbria, Mercia, Kent, East Anglia and Essex.

Whoever controlled the most powerful of these kingdoms was tacitly recognised as overall 'king' – one of the most noted being Alfred the Great, King of Wessex from 871 to 899.

It was during his reign that the famous *Anglo-Saxon Chronicle* was compiled – an invaluable source of Anglo-Saxon history – while Alfred was designated in early documents as *Rex Anglorum Saxonum*, King of the English Saxons.

The Anglo-Saxons, meanwhile, had usurped the power of the indigenous Britons – who referred to them as 'Saeson' or 'Saxones.'

It is from this that the Scottish Gaelic term

for 'English people' of 'Sasannach' derives, the Irish Gaelic 'Sasanach' and the Welsh 'Saeson.'

We learn from the *Anglo-Saxon Chronicle* how the religion of the early Anglo-Saxons was one that pre-dated the establishment of Christianity in the British Isles.

Known as a form of Germanic paganism, with roots in Old Norse religion, it shared much in common with the Druidic 'nature-worshipping' religion of the indigenous Britons.

It was in the closing years of the sixth century that Christianity began to take a hold in Britain, while by approximately 690 it had become the 'established' religion of Anglo-Saxon England.

The first serious shock to Anglo-Saxon control of England came in 789 in the form of sinister black-sailed Viking ships that appeared over the horizon off the island monastery of Lindisfarne, in the northeast of the country.

Lindisfarne was sacked in an orgy of violence and plunder, setting the scene for what would be many more terrifying raids on the coastline of not only England, but also Ireland and Scotland.

But the Vikings, or 'Northmen', in common with the Anglo-Saxons of earlier times, were raiders who eventually stayed – establishing, for example, what became Jorvik, or York, and the trading port of Dublin, in Ireland.

Through intermarriage, the bloodlines of the Anglo-Saxons also became infused with that of the Vikings.

But there would be another infusion of the blood of the 'Northmen' in the wake of the Norman Conquest – a key event in English history that sounded the death knell of Anglo-Saxon supremacy.

By 1066, England had become a nation with several powerful competitors to the throne.

In what were extremely complex family, political and military machinations, the English monarch was Harold II, who had succeeded to the throne following the death of Edward the Confessor.

But his right to the throne was contested by two powerful competitors – his brother-in-law King Harold Hardrada of Norway, in alliance with Tostig, Harold II's brother, and Duke William II of Normandy.

In what has become known as The Year of Three Battles, Hardrada invaded England and gained victory over the English king on September 20 at the battle of Fulford, in Yorkshire.

Five days later, however, Harold II decisively

defeated his brother-in-law and brother at the battle of Stamford Bridge.

But Harold had little time to celebrate his victory, having to immediately march south from Yorkshire to encounter a mighty invasion force, led by Duke William of Normandy that had landed at Hastings, in East Sussex.

Harold's battle-hardened but exhausted force of Anglo-Saxon soldiers confronted the Normans on October 14 in a battle subsequently depicted on the Bayeux tapestry – a 23ft. long strip of embroidered linen thought to have been commissioned eleven years after the event by the Norman Odo of Bayeux.

It was at the top of Senlac Hill that Harold drew up a strong defensive position, building a shield wall to repel Duke William's cavalry and infantry.

The Normans suffered heavy losses, but through a combination of the deadly skill of their archers and the ferocious determination of their cavalry they eventually won the day.

Anglo-Saxon morale had collapsed on the battlefield as word spread through the ranks that Harold had been killed – the Bayeux Tapestry depicting this as having happened when the English king was struck by an arrow to the head.

Amidst the carnage of the battlefield, it was difficult to identify Harold – the last of the Anglo-Saxon kings.

Some sources assert William ordered his body to be thrown into the sea, while others state it was secretly buried at Waltham Abbey.

What is known with certainty, however, is that William in celebration of his great victory founded Battle Abbey, near the site of the battle, ordering that the altar be sited on the spot where Harold was believed to have fallen.

William was declared King of England on December 25, and the complete subjugation of his Anglo-Saxon subjects followed.

Those Normans who had fought on his behalf were rewarded with the lands of Anglo-Saxons, many of whom sought exile abroad as mercenaries.

Within an astonishingly short space of time, Norman manners, customs and law were imposed on England – laying the basis for what subsequently became established 'English' custom and practice.

It was as reward for his assistance to William at the battle of Hastings that the Breton mercenary Robert Fitz-Harvey – sometimes recorded as 'Fitz-Herve' or 'Fitz-Hervey' – was granted lands in Norfolk.

He and his descendants – sometimes confusingly named either 'Harvey' or 'Hervey', to the extent that the names are almost synonymous in the historical record – prospered.

Settling in other geographical areas throughout the British Isles, they gained high honours and distinction over the centuries.

In the original Harvey territory of Norfolk, the Harvey Baronetcy of Crown Point was created in the Baronetage of the United Kingdom in 1868 for Robert Harvey, who had served as Member of Parliament (MP) for Thetford.

In the same family of Harveys, the Harvey Baronetcy of Tasburgh, again in the County of Norfolk, was created in 1954 for the diplomat Sir Oliver Harvey, who had served as British Ambassador to France.

He also later succeeded as 4th Baronet of Crown Point.

Chapter three:

Brave and reckless

Yet another distinguished family of the name – this time in the form of 'Hervey' – is one that since 1826 has held the title of Marquess of Bristol and, for a period before this, also those of Earl of Bristol, Earl Jermyn and Baron Hervey of Ickworth – all in the English county of Suffolk.

This is a highly colourful family who were once memorably summed up in a phrase attributed by some sources to the eighteenth century French philosopher Voltaire.

He stated: *"When God created the human race, he made men, women and Herveys."*

The invaluable reference source the *Dictionary of National Biography* meanwhile refers to their reputation as *"active and brave, but reckless and over-confident … greatly addicted to intrigue."*

With their main residence the Ickworth Estate in Suffolk from the mid-fifteenth century until it was taken over by the National Trust in 1998, the family has certainly produced some noted characters.

Going back to the early sixteenth century, Sir

Nicholas Hervey not only served as Henry VIII's Ambassador to the Holy Roman Emperor but also, with lance in hand took part in jousts at the Field of the Cloth of Gold, near Calais, in 1520.

This was when Henry VIII and Francis I of France staged a glittering tournament featuring their best knights in what proved to be an ultimately unsuccessful attempt to resolve their rival dynastic ambitions through a series of competitive martial contests.

Taking to the high seas, Augustus Hervey, 3rd Earl of Bristol, was the eighteenth century British Admiral renowned not only for his daring actions against the French, but also for romantic intrigues that led to him being known in his time as 'the English Casanova.'

Commander-in Chief of the Mediterranean Fleet in 1763, Hervey Bay, Queensland, was named for him by Captain James Cook in 1770, and also Bristol Bay, in southwest Alaska and Bristol Island in the South Sandwich Islands.

Born in 1724, he died in 1779.

Also at sea, and in a later century, Major Francis Harvey, born in 1873 in Upper Sydenham, Kent, was the British Royal Marine Light Infantry officer who was a posthumous recipient during the First World War of the Victoria Cross (VC) – the highest award for valour in the face of enemy action for British and Commonwealth forces.

A specialist in the art of naval artillery, it was during the battle of Jutland in May of 1916, when the British Grand Fleet clashed in the North Sea with the German High Seas Fleet, that he performed the actions for which he was awarded the honour.

Serving aboard HMS *Lion*, the flagship of the British battle-cruiser fleet, he was mortally wounded by German shellfire when, inside a turret loaded with high explosives and in imminent danger of it exploding, he gave the order for it to be flooded.

His selfless action saved more than 1,000 lives aboard HMS *Lion*, while later paying tribute to him Winston Churchill stated: *"In the long, rough, glorious history of the Royal Marines there is no name and no deed which in its character and consequences ranks above this."*

Returning to the Hervey family, namesakes of the equally noted Harveys, Frederick Augustus Hervey, also known as the Earl-Bishop, served as Bishop of Cloyne, in Ireland, from 1767 to 1768 and as Bishop of Derry from 1768 to 1803.

Known to his contemporaries as *"the most worldly, most eccentric, most talked about priest in the Church of Ireland"*, he not only used his considerable wealth to build magnificent personal residences, but also in acts of philanthropy that included agricultural improvements and road building.

On one occasion, while considering which of his ambitious priests should be promoted to a particularly lucrative position, he resolved the issue by making them engage in a gruelling and competitive midnight run through swamps and bogs.

Born in 1730, he died in 1803.

One particularly flamboyant member of the aristocratic Hervey family was Victor Hervey, 6th Marquess of Bristol, who was born in 1906.

Dubbed in his youth by the Press as 'Mayfair's Number One Playboy', he was the leader of a group of similar dissolute and young aristocrats known as the Mayfair Playboys.

Jailed for three years for his part in two jewellery robberies in the Mayfair district of London when he was aged 22, he had already been declared bankrupt with debts estimated at a staggering £5.93m in today's terms.

Recouping his wealth through property

interests and other business deals and a patron of the International Monarchist League, he died in tax exile in Monaco in 1985.

He was the father, through his marriage to Yvonne Marie Sutton, of the English socialite and model Lady Victoria Hervey.

Born in 1976 and the older sister of Frederick Hervey, 8th Marquess of Bristol, she has been romantically linked in the past to celebrities who include Scottish former Formula One racing driver David Coulthard.

One bearer of the proud name of Harvey whose important legacy survives to this day in the medical world was the English physician William Harvey, recognised as having been the first to have accurately described in detail the systematic circulation of blood pumped through the body by the heart.

Born in 1578 in Folkestone, the son of the town mayor, it was when he was aged 24 that he graduated as a doctor of medicine from the University of Padua, in Italy.

Returning to his native England and obtaining further medical qualifications through the University of Cambridge, in 1628 he published his famous treatise on the circulation of blood, *De Motu Cordis* – also known as *On the Motion of the Heart and Blood*.

Having earlier been appointed Physician Extraordinary to King James I (James VI) of Scotland and later as physician to successor Charles I, he died in 1657.

The William Harvey Hospital in the town of Ashford, near his birthplace of Folkestone, was later founded and named in his honour.

Chapter four:

On the world stage

Born in 1969 in Bridport, Dorset, Polly Jean Harvey is the multi-award-winning English singer and songwriter better known as PJ Harvey.

Her 2001 *Stories from the City, Stories from the Sea* won the Mercury Award for Best Album, as did her 2011 *Let England Shake* – making her the first artist to be awarded the prize twice.

Named by *Rolling Stone* magazine in 1995 as its Artist of the Year, she was awarded for Outstanding Contribution to Music at the *New Musical Express (NME)* Awards in 2011.

Born in 1935 in the Kinning Park area of Glasgow, **Alex Harvey** was the Scottish blues and rock musician who, along with The Sensational Alex Harvey Band, enjoyed hits that include the 1976 *The Boston Tea Party*.

He died in 1982, while his brother Les Harvey, born in 1944 and who was the guitarist with the band Stone the Crows, died after being electrocuted on stage in 1972.

Sacked as lead singer of the band East 17

after making controversial comments in a radio interview concerning the use of the drug Ecstasy, **Brian Harvey** is the English singer and musician born in 1974 in Walthamstow, London.

He later re-joined the band, which was renamed E-17.

Born in Plymouth in 1979, Michael Harvey is the musician, actor and television personality better known as **MC Harvey**.

Now enjoying a successful solo career since 2008 after being a member of the British rap group So Solid Crew, he also has film credits that include the 2010 *The Big I Am*.

Formerly married to the singer Alesha Dixon, he also played for a time in English non-league football for teams that include Wimbledon, Lewes and Aldershot Town.

Author of a number of acclaimed works on music that include his 1975 *The Music of Stockhausen: An Introduction*, **Jonathan Harvey** was the British composer born in 1939 in Sutton Coldfield.

A cellist for a time with the BBC Scottish Symphony Orchestra, his many other professional posts before his death in 2012 included, from 2005 to 2008, Composer in Association for the orchestra.

From music to the stage, Zvi Mosheh Skikne was the Lithuanian-born actor better known as **Laurence Harvey**.

Born in 1928 and immigrating with his family when he was aged five to South Africa, he served during the Second World War with an entertainment unit of the South African Army.

Moving to Britain at the end of the conflict and studying at the London Academy of Dramatic Art, he later gained acclaim for his lead role of Joe Lampton in the 1959 film *Room at the Top*.

Receiving both a BAFTA Award nomination and an Academy Award nomination for Best Actor for his performance in *Room at the Top*, his other notable film credits include the 1955 *I Am a Camera* and the 1961 *The Long and the Short and the Tall*.

Married for a time to the actress Margaret Leighton, he died in 1973.

Not only an actor but also a writer and producer, Harvey Ainsworth Hilton, better known by his professional name of **Frank Harvey**, was born in 1885 in Earls Court, London. A stage actor before turning to film, his big screen credits include the 1931 *Cape Forlorn* and the 1938 *The Broken Melody*, both based on his own screenplays.

He died in 1965, while he was also the father of the English screenwriter also known as **Frank Harvey**.

Born in Manchester in 1912, it was along with John Boulting and Alan Hackney that he won a BAFTA Award for screenwriting for the 1960 British film *I'm All Right Jack*.

Other noted films for which he wrote the screenplays include the 1956 *Private's Progress* and, from 1957, *Brothers in Law*; he died in 1981.

Born in 1924 in Windsor, Colorado, **Harold Harvey** was the American actor, director and producer best known for his cult 1962 horror film *Carnival of Souls*; he died in 1996.

Starting his career as a film editor and later moving into directing, **Anthony Harvey** is the British filmmaker born in London in 1931.

As a director, his credits include the 1968 *The Lion in Winter*, for which he won a Directors Guild of America Award and an Academy Award nomination, and the 1985 *Grace Quigley*.

His film editing credits include the 1962 *Lolita*, starring James Mason, and the 1965 *The Spy Who Came In from the Cold*, starring Richard Burton.

Bearers of the Harvey name have also excelled,

and continue to excel, in the highly competitive world of sport.

On the cricket pitch, **The Harvey Brothers** dominated the game in Australia from the early to the mid-decades of the twentieth century.

From Victoria, they are Merv, born in 1918 and who died in 1995; Mick, born in 1921; Harold, born in 1923; Ray, born in 1926; Neil, born in 1928 and Brian, born in 1932 and who died in 1969.

Although all six brothers, who played for Melbourne's Fitzroy Club – now the Fitzroy-Doncasters – were noted players in their own right, the most noted is **Neil Harvey**.

Regarded by the cricketing authority *Wisden* as the leading fielder in the world during his career and having played 79 Test matches for Australia between 1948 and 1963, he is an inductee of the Australian Cricket Hall of Fame and the International Cricket Council (ICC) Cricket Hall of Fame.

His brother Merv Harvey was the grandfather of the former Australian rules footballer **Robert Harvey**, born in 1971 and who, having played for the St Kilda Football Club in the Australian Football League (AFL), has been ranked as one of the league's top midfielders of the modern era.

On the fields of European football, **Colin Harvey**, born in Liverpool in 1944, is the retired midfielder who, in addition to playing for the England national team in 1971, also managed Everton from 1987 to 1990.

As a player, he was with Everton from 1963 to 1974, while he also played for Sheffield Wednesday from 1974 to 1976.

Born in Leeds in 1948, **David Harvey** is the goalkeeper who, in addition to having played for teams that include Leeds United also qualified, through his paternal roots, to play for Scotland from 1972 to 1976.

From football to the Canadian national sport of ice hockey, **Doug Harvey**, born in Montreal in 1924, played for teams in the National Hockey League (NHL) from 1945 to 1969 that include the Montreal Canadiens, New York Rangers and Quebec Aces.

An inductee of the Hockey Hall of Fame, he was also honoured eleven years after his death in 1989 with his image on a Canadian postage stamp.

In martial arts, **Michael Harvey**, born in 1989 in Hyde, Greater Manchester is the British practitioner of the discipline of taekwondo who won a silver medal at the 2011 World Championships and gold at the 2012 European Championships.

From sport to the creative world of the written word, **Francis Harvey** is the Irish poet and playwright born in 1925 in Enniskillen, Co. Fermanagh.

Winner of the 1989 Guardian and World Wildlife Fund Poetry Competition for his poem *Heron*, his other works include the 1978 collection *In the Light on the Stones* and the 1996 *The Boa Island Janus*.

In the equally creative world of art and illustration, **Alfred Harvey** was the creator of the highly popular comic book publisher *Harvey World Famous Comics* and comic book characters who include *Wendy the Good Little Witch*, *Baby Huey*, *Little Audrey* and *Casper the Friendly Ghost*.

Born in 1913, he died in 1994 – five years after his company was sold to HMH Communications and renamed *Harvey Comics Entertainment*.

In the world of invention, **Hayward Harvey**, born in 1824 in Jamestown, New York and who died in 1893, was the industrialist who invented what is known as the Harvey process for case-hardening the front surface of steel-armoured plate, mainly used on battleships.

Bearers of the Harvey name have also founded leading business enterprises.

Famed to this day as the Bristol-based importers and bottlers of Spanish and Portuguese wines and whose products include Bristol Cream Sherry, the company of **John Harvey and Sons** was started in Bristol by John Harvey in 1796.

The brand is now owned by the American company Beam Incorporated.

Founded in London originally as a linen shop by **Benjamin Harvey** in 1831 in a terraced house on the corner of Sloane Street and Knightsbridge, **Harvey Nichols** is now an international chain of department stores.

It was when his daughter took over the business that, in partnership with a Colonel Nichols, the business became known as what is today's upmarket brand of Harvey Nichols.

In Australia, **Gerry Harvey** is the leading entrepreneur who, along with Ian Norman, founded the retail chain of **Harvey Norman**.

Born in 1939 in Bathurst, New South Wales, at the time of writing he is ranked at 13th in the list of the richest people in Australia.

One particularly innovative and enterprising

bearer of the proud name of Harvey was Frederick Henry Harvey, better known as **Fred Harvey**.

Born of mixed English and Scottish parentage in London in 1835 and immigrating to the United States at the age of 17, he is credited with having created the nation's first restaurant chains.

Working as a humble pot scrubber in a New York restaurant, he later moved to New Orleans and started a café business.

By 1873, he had launched a much more ambitious enterprise that eventually led to the setting up of a highly profitable string of **Harvey House** lunch rooms, restaurants, hotels and souvenir shops that served rail passengers on networks that included the Kansas Pacific Railway, the Gulf Coast and Santa Fe Railway and the Atchison, Topeka and Santa Fe Railway.

His enterprise was renowned for good value for money – but Harvey, nevertheless, always had a very careful eye on how to trim costs where possible to maximise profit.

On his deathbed in 1901, surrounded by his sons who were set to take over his business, his final words were: *"Cut the ham thinner, boys."*

Now part of a much larger American

hospitality industry conglomerate, Harvey's original company, which employed waitresses known as Harvey Girls, was the subject of the 1946 film musical *The Harvey Girls*, starring Judy Garland, Cyd Charisse and Angela Lansbury.